Creating Sacred Space

The Art of Living an Abundant &
Peaceful Life… Sacred Ceremonies
for Women Who Do Too Much.

Cyndi Harris, HP

For ordering, booking, permission, or questions, contact the author.

Cyndi Harris

email: Cyndi@redtentwisdom.com

website: www.redtentwisdom.com

ISBN-13:978-1499504675

Printed in the United States of America by Create Space

DEDICATION

This book is dedicated to my three incredible and wonderful sons, Michael, Anthony, and Christopher; who remind me how precious life is and how grateful I am to have such wonderful young men in my life. We have been through much over the years and they know the value of faith and prayer along with determination and the importance of never giving up on your dreams.

And I am also dedicating this book to the amazing and inspirational women I have the pleasure and privilege of knowing as friends, clients, and mentors. Each of you inspires me more than simple words will ever express.

Thank you!

CONTENTS

Introduction

Creating Sacred Space & Sacred Ceremonies

"Silence is the language of God, all else is poor translation." - Rumi

Creating sacred space and performing sacred ceremonies is all about allowing yourself to disconnect from the noise and frantic energy of our daily lives. The constant need to be on the phone, internet, tweeting, instagram, and other distractions has made it difficult for many people to relax and be at peace with silence or even spend quality time connecting with loved ones.

How many times have you sat down to a meal and everyone comes to the table with a cell phone or computer? It is becoming more and more difficult to put away the gadgets and enjoy life. All this **"noise"** is creating chaos which seems to be adding to the dysfunction of even the most basic moments of our days.

And there is no way to get away from it unless you make an active commitment to do so. The ceremonies in this book have been designed to bring back the peace and joy of focused and peaceful celebration; tapping into your heart and soul's memory of a happier and more precious time in our lives that makes us smile, relax, and enjoy restoration.

Or if you have never truly known peace then, this book will provide you with the guidance and steps to bring peace into your life and leave the past where it belongs... a distant memory.

Why am I writing this as a series? For several reasons, mainly to because I believe in the K.I.S.S. theory... Keep It Simple Sweetie. I personally prefer to read information that cuts out the excess and gets to the point of what I am learning. Quality over quantity is my mission.

Why and how do I feel this book will benefit you? Well, let me ask you one very important question. Have you noticed, you never feel there is enough time to fulfill all of the obligations in your life and overwhelm is your constant companion? I know so many people who seem on the surface to be functioning just fine amongst the chaos.

But, one day something happens. An unexpected event or expectation is their undoing. They fall apart; emotionally, mentally, physically, or spiritually. It is only when they have begun to embrace the importance of silence and personal care do they appreciate how much being alone, in meditation or prayer, or just enjoying some gadget free time with loved ones do they understand that life is about the quality of your time; not quantity of tasks you can fit into your day.

This series is a simple way to answer questions, offer guidelines, and helpful hints and ideas to enhance the quality of your life. Once you begin to practice the tips offered in this book and the additional books in this series; the people around you will benefit as well.

Now, if you are uncertain about adding sacred ceremonies to your life; ask yourself the following questions:

- Is the stress of your life destroying your health? (Acid reflux, headaches, indigestion, body aches/joint pain, and possibly more serious conditions.)
- Are your personal relationships suffering due to your lack of focus, free time, and ability to relax and be present with the people who love you?
- Is your peace of mind a distant memory?
- Has all of the mayhem caused you to disconnect from your personal joy?
- Do you feel guilty if you try to put the gadgets away and just enjoy some peace and quiet?
  - o Are you worried that you might miss something?
  - o Does this cause anxiety or obsessive compulsions?

These are just a few of the symptoms that manifest a chaotic life.

Consider your answers to the above questions a wakeup call; a call to action that brings you peace of mind and more personal enjoyment if you choose to follow the guidelines offered in this book. Inside you will discover ways to reestablish inner peace and the pleasure of living a serene and on purpose life minus the endless "noise".

Serenity is the key word and idea of enjoying ceremonies created for your pleasure and to reacquaint you with its presence in your life.

Before you start performing any of the ceremonies; I recommend you look through the book from beginning to end to be sure you have the recommended tools you need to fully enjoy the experiences outlined with each meditation/prayer.

Allow yourself to fully engage in these moments; set an appointment with yourself to be certain no one will disturb you. Also, be sure to give yourself 30 – 45 minutes to relax and really allow this sacred experience to sink in and become a part of your personal vibration.

Ideally, you should do something special each day. If not possible, you should schedule at least 3 sessions/week.

Sacred Wisdom # 1:

100% Commitment to your sacred practice is important. Consistency will ground the vibration of your desire in your personal energy and allow the Divine to step up and fulfill your personal requests.

Devoting yourself 100% to your daily practice will unlock your personal blessings in the most profound and unexpected ways. One of the reasons most goals or requests fail is; we keep running "hot and cold" about what we are seeking.

At first, it seems easy because of the initial excitement you feel around your request. Unfortunately, as time goes by and nothing immediately happens; you feel a little discouraged. Then, add in other people's opinions and their lack of enthusiasm for your personal desires and determination to receive them. Your energy starts to drop and doubt begins to set in. Then, you decide you will ignore the naysayers and hold on to your belief in your vision. Unfortunately, while the waiting continues for something to happen you feel your faith begin to falter once again.

So, the next thing you know; you are up and down when it comes to fulfilling your desires and dreams. This indecisive trend unconsciously locks you into a downward spiral which seems impossible to release.

Well, the antidote to this dilemma is to **commit 100% to realization of your desires**; be willing to commit sight unseen to the very things you dream about, talk about, and fill your fantasies.

One of the ways to keep this flow of intention strong is to honor the need for sacred space to indulge in your sacred ceremonies; a place where you can go to reconnect to the Divine and solidify your personal relationship with the creator of all abundance, perfect health, peace of mind, and wealth.

Sacred ceremonies can really bridge the gap between modern technology and the hyper energy it generates to the peaceful singularly focused joy that can be found in carefully planning time each day to honor the Divine within and around you.

Also, the guidelines I share with you in this book are strictly based on the spiritual practice that I have enjoyed for many years and the pleasure and serenity it has brought me, my family, and clients. You will find a variety of options to use as support for your meditations and prayers. I truly do honor the various paths people select to achieve a personal relationship with their interpretation of God. The information in this book has been provided to enhance your personal practice and possibly offer you some options you where previously unaware of.

So, have fun with the process and while collecting the tools you will need to fully embrace and personalize these spiritual gifts for your enjoyment.

You are in for a wonderful surprise. And remember, consistency is very important. I suggest you use the space for journaling on your worksheet. The worksheets provide the following information:

- Candle Colors (Appendix 1 covers their specific meanings)

- Suggested incenses and essential oil options.

- A space to write in your favorite angel or spirit guide.

- Mantras to keep you focused on your intentions.

- Plus, space to write what comes to mind while you are meditating or praying.

Plus, I have included a section called: **"Something to Think About"**; which offers a variety of inspirational quotes.

As you embrace the ideas in this book, you will notice new things happening in your life and your journal notes will be a huge help in remembering the blessings that are showing up in your life.

 At first, the changes may be very subtle, but as you continue to enjoy these private and sacred ceremonies; you will one day look up and see that your entire life has changed for the better. You will manifest with ease, love will seem deeper and more satisfying, and personal happiness will be a constant part of your daily endeavors.

I know firsthand how it feels to wake up each morning excited about the upcoming day. I am thankful for the opportunity to share this same pleasure with you.

Let's begin.

Chapter 1: Creating Magical and Mystical Space

Magical and mystical space sounds pleasant doesn't it? When I started writing this chapter, I was looking around my living room and thinking about how precious this space is to me. I have several of my favorite crystals, gemstones, and pictures scattered throughout the room.

In one corner is my main altar where I sit in the mornings and sometimes in the evenings to meditate and do mantras or prayers. There are candles burning on the altar; the colors vary depending on the prayer requests I have expressed.

On the altar, there are also pictures and beautiful gemstones and quartz crystals along with my prayer beads hanging on the wall.

Adding to the beauty of my altar, I keep a gorgeous lead cut crystal glass filled with sea salt to hold my incenses; which I light at different times of the day to enhance my home's ambiance. I love the smell of incense. They add a very comforting and peaceful feeling that people always notice.

My clients and guests tell me how relaxing it feels to sit in this room. I know they speak the truth because, I enjoy sitting in this room as well either on the couch or at my altar comfortably meditating, praying, or spending time in quiet reflection about my day. Plus, it is a wonderful place to conduct the prayers that I do for others as well.

The creation of this holy and sacred space elevates the feelings and emotions I bring to it. Knowing this, I do my best to begin my meditation or prayer in an positive and uplifted state of mind.

Sometimes this is not my reality, but I know that once I do sit down with a concern, my state of mind will alter for the better since I am surrounded by the loving energy of this loving place in my home.

Now, it is your turn to set aside a special place in your house for peaceful reflection. It is your turn to provide a beautiful and special place for you to joyfully enjoy your personal meditation and prayers.

Sacred space is a wonderful gift I believe each person should provide for themselves and share with others in the home. Your pets will even enjoy the loving and holy feeling of your personal spot.

It will become your special haven that reinforces your commitment to sit to meditate, pray, or reflect; feeling the richness of the energy and uplifting vibrations you are creating. You will begin to notice how pleasantly different this special space feels from the rest of your house.

This sacred space will give you a place to go and surrender your daily concerns and eventually receive a true sense of peace and possibilities.

So, you are asking how do I set this space up? What do I need? How do I set up an altar? It is actually easier than most people realize. Nearly any surface large enough to hold a picture, gemstones, candle, and incense can be used as an altar. It can be as simple or elaborate as you envision. I personally use end tables that I have selected to hold the very beautiful and personal items I mentioned earlier in this chapter; pictures, crystals/gemstones, candles, incenses, and a variety of other items that have special meaning to me and my spiritual practice.

So, how do you set up an altar? It is very simple. The following steps should help.

1. **Find a table that is large enough to hold:**
   a. A couple of pictures of yourself, family members, angels, ascended masters, etc.,
   b. 2 – 3 candles
   c. An incense holder or crystal glass filled with sea salt to hold the incense stick and catch the ashes
   d. And a few gemstones.

     e. I also use prayer beads during my meditations. So, I make sure I have a wall where I can put a cup hook large enough to hang my beads when I am not using them.

2. **If you like you may cover the table with a beautiful piece of cloth.** This is totally personal preference. I do not use any type of cloth. **I prefer to use beautiful marble tiles instead.** I like the tiles because some of my ceremonies require me to burn candles for several days uninterrupted. The tiles provide me with a lovely fireproof surface.

3. **Pick a place in your home where you can setup your altar undisturbed.** I realize if you have children or pets this may be a bit of a challenge. If this is the case you may decide to use a portable altar instead.

     a. A portable altar is the stuff listed above, but instead of leaving it in one place you store your items in a beautiful container that you can place out of the reach of curious little ones when not in use.

4. **Once you have selected where you are going to setup your altar clear the space using a "Space Clearing" prayer (I have included one in this book)** and sage or use incense to cleanse the old energies and prepare the space to become your personal space. You want to say the prayer as you are walking throughout the room allowing the smoke of the sage or incense to fill the room. **Be sure to get into the corners since energy has a way of getting stuck in them.**

5. **Now that you have cleansed the space,** you can set up your altar. Take all of the things you have gathered and begin placing them on your altar. There are specific ways you can setup an altar, I will save those for a more advanced book.

     a. **Today, I want you to focus on how it feels to place your items on your altar.** Use your intuition/spiritual guidance and start to get a "feel" for your personal space.

b. **Once done, say a prayer of thanks for the guidance, light a white candle and just sit for a moment enjoying your new space.** As you use this space, you will begin to notice a very pleasant change in you and those around you.

Chapter 2: Types of sacred ceremonies

Being grateful for each of life's miracles and moments of your life; no matter how big or small, sets you up for even greater blessings. This one of the reasons a gratitude practice is an important part of your daily routine." – Rev. Cyndi Harris

Ceremonies can be so much fun, add polish, and purpose to our lives. Think about the various religious or spiritual celebrations and events that take place around the world; especially during the holidays. A Catholic mass comes to mind; all of the pomp and circumstance; candles, incense, the prayers/incantation, etc.

Or how about the day to day act of living, the minor ceremonies we do without thinking about them. For example, when you light a scented candle before your guests arrive for a special get together to sweeten the smell of your home; unconsciously you know the fragrance will become part everyone's happy memories of the time they will spend in your home and with you. You feel a little excited and a certain sense of reverence. You feel honorable and sacred as you light the candle. This is a very simple example of a sacred mini ceremony.

When you stop and take a moment to think about your life. You will realize your day is filled with a variety of rituals and routines. Generally, we all have a special process to our morning routine. And, if we get up late, our whole morning can become hectic mess that sets the "feeling" for the rest our day.

You have a certain place you grab your morning coffee or meal. You eat at a certain place, dress and shop from certain stores, drive a certain way to work every morning, etc. I could go on, but I am sure you understand what I am bringing to your attention. We are creatures of habits. We do plenty of things throughout our day that contribute to the dull and mundane moments of our day. We also do plenty of things that add to the stress and dissatisfaction too.

Becoming aware of these daily patterns and knowing you have the option to change the things that no longer serve your best interests and needs; can be very helpful.

Starting today, consciously decide to do something that makes you feel good and offers you time to:

- Gather your thoughts
- Remember and manifest your dreams
- And create an environment of relaxation and peace in your home.

Sacred Wisdom # 2:

Ideally, your home should be the one place you can go to escape the hassle and hustle of sharing the world with others. Your home is the place you can create the type of quality living you may not enjoy elsewhere. Your home is supposed to be your safe haven; if not, it should be. And the best way to be sure it is a happy place is to plan for it.

Here is one of the beautiful things about embracing the sacred nature of your home is; once you have set up your meditation and prayer area. It might encourage you to allow more room in your life for the type of ceremonies which will add to the joy and pleasure of your home. Ceremonies can be used to:

- Celebrate happy life events
- Manifest money
- Recover from an illness
- Calm down after a hectic day
- Celebrate romance
- Invite love and romance into your life
- Recover from loss (Break up of a relationship, someone passing away, etc.)
- Encourage peace of mind

It becomes fun and if you live with others; they will want to help you maintain the sanctity of your home.

Eventually, as you become more comfortable and at peace in your home; you will find more and more reasons to celebrate, heal, and rejoice. To help you move through the book more easily. I have divided the ceremonies and prayers into separate sections; focus on the ones which meet your specific need. Also, the worksheets are provided to keep things simple and sweet. If you have any questions; feel free to contact me at **www.redtentwisdom.com**.

Chapter 3 – Prosperity Prayers

"You are Divine royalty. Remember who you are and prepare to allow then, receive the heavenly abundance that is your birthright." – Rev. Cyndi Harris, HP

Now, as you begin to explore the following prayers and fill in the worksheets. Remember, this is all about you. The prayers and guidelines are here to assist you and make the inclusion of your designated daily personal time easier to create.

Most people feel overwhelmed by the variety of options and at times rigid practices available in our modern age. So, they continue to find excuses to ignore the need in their life for such a sacred practice. My goal in this book is to remind you to have fun and create excitement around this special gift you are offering yourself.

Yes, maintaining a daily spiritual practice requires discipline, but the benefits will outweigh any difficulties you may perceive in the beginning. By reading this book and utilizing its offerings you will be opening your life up to more of the good things you dream about. Following the guidelines and being more present in your day to day process sets you up to allow then, receive the very things that currently seem so elusive and out of reach in the current chaos of your life.

Remember, by remaining committed to this daily practice. You are replenishing your spirit and energizing your life. This newfound energy and peace of mind will bring more abundance, love, joy, and pleasure into your day to day existence. So, go for it!

Have fun with it and allow the universe to take better care of you.

Also, for those who are unfamiliar with the phrase **"So mote it be". It is simply means: "The truth has been spoken or so it must be".** Basically, it is another way of ending a prayer in a positive and respectful way. Here is your first prayer.

"Calling in Your Blessings"

North, East, South, and West

My heavenly parents, I pray you will favorably answer my humble request.

I pray you will provide the following, (your request), to me.

My request brings harm to none in body, mind or soul.

I gladly give my thanks to Thee.

This is my prayer so mote it be.

Amen

Cyndi Harris, HP - Red Tent Wisdom 2011© Revised 2014

Cyndi's Suggestions:

To really enjoy the full benefits of this beautiful prayer; I recommend you:

- Go into your bedroom and light 2 white candles to start the relaxation process.
- Light some incense or use your diffuser with your favorite essential oil to fragrance your room.
- Turn on your favorite cd or ipod playlist that encourages you to relax and prepare yourself mentally for your upcoming time of communion.
- Also light candles, incense/essential oil diffuser, and music in your bathroom as well.
- Take a shower with your most luxurious and beautifully-scented shower gel to wash off the grunge and negative energy of your day.
- Dry yourself with a pretty big fluffy towel that you reserve for your special showers before prayer or meditation.
- Massage yourself from head to toe with scented lotion or oil to soften your skin while thinking about how good you feel and wonderful you smell.
- Once done slip into a special outfit that is comfortable enough to sit in for your sacred time.

Now, you are ready to proceed.

Something to Think About:

"To will is to select a goal, determine a course of action that will bring one to that goal, then hold to that action till the goal is reached. The key is action." – Anais Nin

Candles: (Color)	Green, Green Yellow, Orange (Depends on the day)
Incense:	**Suggestions:** **Essential Essences: Frankincense and Myrrh** – "Consecration and Healing" **Essential Essences: Prosperity** – Cinnabar & Cinnamon **Satya Sai Baba:** Nag Champa Agarbatti Your Personal Favorite:
Essential Oil/s	Frankincense, Myrrh
Moon Cycle:	New moon to the day before full moon
Angel/Spirit Guide:	
Mantras:	
	"I Am wealthy. I Am wealth."
	"I love money & money loves me; I graciously and gratefully receive."
Notes: (Share your thoughts below)	

"Unlimited Abundance and Financial Prayer"

Air, Earth, Wind, and Rain

I say this prayer to welcome into my life unlimited abundance and financial gain.

The riches and wealth I receive will cause no one any; emotional, mental, physical, or spiritual pain.

The ability to withdraw from the unlimited universal riches and supply

Is a gift I am grateful for and am thankful my request you will never deny.

My request is to receive the financial blessing and gift of (state your financial request).

The financial gift of (your request) has been placed in my hands, giving life to my dream and its immediate start.

This is my prayer, so mote it be.

Amen

Cyndi Harris, HP - Red Tent Wisdom 2011© Revised 2014

Cyndi's Suggestions:

To really enjoy the full benefits of this beautiful prayer; I recommend you:

- Go into your bedroom and light 2 white candles to start the relaxation process.
- Light some incense or use your diffuser with your favorite essential oil to fragrance your room.
- Turn on your favorite cd or ipod playlist that encourages you to relax and prepare yourself mentally for your upcoming time of communion.
- Also light candles, incense/essential oil diffuser, and music in your bathroom as well.
- Take a shower with your most luxurious and beautifully-scented shower gel to wash off the grunge and negative energy of your day.
- Dry yourself with a pretty big fluffy towel that you reserve for your special showers before prayer or meditation.
- Massage yourself from head to toe with scented lotion or oil to soften your skin while thinking about how good you feel and wonderful you smell.
- Once done slip into a special outfit that is comfortable enough to sit in for your sacred time.

Now, you are ready to proceed.

Something to Think About:

"What you seek is seeking you." - Rumi

Candles: (Color)	Green, Green Yellow, Orange (Depends on the day)
Incense:	**Suggestions:** **Essential Essences: Frankincense and Myrrh** – "Consecration and Healing" **Essential Essences: Prosperity** – Cinnabar & Cinnamon **Satya Sai Baba:** Nag Champa Agarbatti Your Personal Favorite:
Essential Oil/s	Frankincense, Myrrh
Moon Cycle:	New moon to the day before full moon
Angel/Spirit Guide:	
Mantras:	
	"I Am wealthy. I Am wealth."
	"I love money & money loves me; I graciously and gratefully receive."
Notes: (Share your thoughts below)	

Chapter 4 - Spacing Clearing Prayer

Why am I including a prayer for space cleansing? Because, just like us, our home collects the energy that people bring into it. Arguments, depression, laughter, joy, etc. collects in the walls, furniture, carpet/floors, and every other surface; your home becomes an emotion-filled "mirror" of the people and events taking place within.

Plus, if a house blessing or cleansing was not done before you moved in; you have inherited the energy of the home's previous owners. You now are the recipient of all their emotional issues, highs, and lows as well. The same is true for items handed down through your family's legacy or any new or used items you have purchased and brought into your home.

If you are unsure about the correctness of the above paragraph; think about the time you went to visit someone after an argument took place in their home. You walk in the door and can feel the tension in the air. Or how about a historical place you may have visited while on vacation.

I personally had an experience at Valley Forge as a teenager that discourages me from wanting to return. The energy at Valley Forge is hopeless, sad, and very depressing. As it should be since the poor souls that spent their winters there during the Revolutionary War were unhappy and endured many unpleasant experiences. Their energy is embedded in the walls of the cabins that still remain and even in the ground. Since, I am so sensitive to energy. The sadness was the first thing I noticed. Even after hundreds of years the energy is still present.

Now, please understand, not all energy left behind in a location is depressing, sad, or angry. I have been inside places where the energy was fun, peaceful, and pleasant. In my hometown, we have a country club that is housed in building whose former history is spiritually based. You walk through the heavy wood doors into the lobby and instantly relax.

So, realizing the importance of energetically cleansing your home periodically is very essential to the well-being of you and your loved ones. You want your home to be a place of peace, love, and joy. Use the following prayer as a seasonal energetic reboot for your home.

Here is a simple space clearing ritual:

The Salt Burn Space Cleansing Ceremony

Salt is a natural way to absorb negative energy and promote healing. One of the great things about salt is it can be used in a very simple ritual to cleanse your personal or professional space. Burning salt is a powerful way to send unwanted energy on its way.

You will need:

- 1 fireproof container (A ceramic mug is fine. You can throw the mug away once the salt is done burning and the mug is cool to touch)

- A fire safe place to place the mug during the ceremony. (A marble tile, glass block square, or a cast iron or stainless steel skillet will work just fine.)

- Epsom or sea salt

- An unopened bottle of high alcohol content alcohol (Bacardi rum 151 is a good selection.)

- Matches

The Ceremony:

Once you have assembled all your tools take a few deep breaths to clear your mind and ground your energy.

- Recite the following space clearing prayer.

- Place the coffee mug on your fire-safe tile, glass block, or skillet.

- Fill the palm of your hand with the salt and pour the salt into the mug. (Do this 3 times.)

- Pour just enough of the alcohol you selected to cover the salt.

- Light match and drop it into the mixture.

While the mixture is burning, visualize any negative, heavy, or unpleasant energies being absorbed by the fire then, being transformed into positive and productive energy or simply leaving your space.

To enhance the positive vibration being created by the burning salt; think about how you wish to use this space. Think happy, pleasant, and prosperous thoughts. Say a special mantra or prayer that will increase the good energy in this space.

When the salt burns out, let the mug cool down, and remove it from your home or office and dispose of it in your outdoor trash container. Or, if you decide to reuse the mug; chip out the salt residue and flush it down the toilet.

Either way, you must dispose of the salt residue since it contains the negative energy you just removed from your home or office.

And this completes our simple, but effective space clearing ceremony/ritual. Use it whenever you notice the energy in your home or office is becoming unpleasant or unproductive.

Once you done this a few times and enjoyed the uplifting feeling of your newly cleansed space. You will seek other spaces to clear.

Enjoy!

"Space Clearing"

Earth, Wind, Fire, and Air

Please, help me clear this space I pray.

Bring into this space happy, healing, joyful energy and love.

And all negativity, I am asking you to erase and immediately eliminate.

Keeping it safe and pleasant for my clients/family/friends and me.

This is my prayer, so mote it be.

Amen

Cyndi Harris, HP - Red Tent Wisdom 2011© Revised 2014

Cyndi's Suggestions:

To really enjoy the full benefits of this beautiful prayer; I recommend you:

- Go into your bedroom and light 2 white candles to start the relaxation process.
- Light some incense or use your diffuser with your favorite essential oil to fragrance your room.
- Turn on your favorite cd or ipod playlist that encourages you to relax and prepare yourself mentally for your upcoming time of communion.
- Also light candles, incense/essential oil diffuser, and music in your bathroom as well.
- Take a shower with your most luxurious and beautifully-scented shower gel to wash off the grunge and negative energy of your day.
- Dry yourself with a pretty big fluffy towel that you reserve for your special showers before prayer or meditation.
- Massage yourself from head to toe with scented lotion or oil to soften your skin while thinking about how good you feel and wonderful you smell.
- Once done slip into a special outfit that is comfortable enough to sit in for your sacred time.

Now, you are ready to proceed.

Something to Think About:

"When you feel peaceful joy, that's when you are near truth." - Rumi

Candles: (Color)	White & Black
Incense:	**Suggestions:** **Essential Essences: Sacred Cedar and Lavender** – "Purification" **Satya Sai Baba:** Nag Champa Agarbatti Your Personal Favorite:
Essential Oil/s	Frankincense, Myrrh
Moon Cycle:	Full moon to the day before new moon
Angel/Spirit Guide:	
Mantras:	
	"I Am living in a happy and sacred space."
	"I Am the fulfillment of my best dreams & intentions."
Notes: (Share your thoughts below)	

Chapter 5 - Love/Romance Prayers

Prayers for love and romance are some of my favorite to create. The energy of love has so many emotions, expectations, highs and lows attached to it. We feel love, crave love, and live to love and be loved.

Unfortunately, there are also times we will self-sabotage the love in our lives. The past and sometimes the fears and limitations of others, when we allow it, create conflicts in our love life too. Allowing yourself to get caught up in the expectations of others can, over time, turn you into a self-fulfilling prophecy which constantly creates havoc in your love life.

So, in the following prayers I have included a variety of options to meet several situations that occur in our love lives. Situations like:

- Self-appreciation
- Calling in a new love relationship
- Forgiveness
- Letting go of the past
- Reestablishing love
- Surrendering to the sweetness of love and romance
- Etc.

Each prayer was designed to help you reflect on the pleasure of love and its many expressions. To empower you and offer you words of sacred wisdom to move past the disappointment and pain of love relationships that have ended; releasing the stale and stuck energy which inhibits your ability to start over in a better place.

I hope you enjoy these special prayers as much as I enjoyed creating them and using them myself.

Here's to the power of Love.

"I AM Loving/I AM Loved"

I AM loving and I AM loved,

True joy and happiness flow through me from Divine love above.

I AM at peace and all things come to me with the greatest of ease.

This is my prayer. So mote it be.

Amen

Cyndi Harris, HP - Red Tent Wisdom 2011©

Cyndi's Suggestions:

To really enjoy the full benefits of this beautiful prayer; I recommend you:

- Go into your bedroom and light 2 white candles to start the relaxation process.
- Light some incense or use your diffuser with your favorite essential oil to fragrance your room.
- Turn on your favorite cd or ipod playlist that encourages you to relax and prepare yourself mentally for your upcoming time of communion.
- Also light candles, incense/essential oil diffuser, and music in your bathroom as well.
- Take a shower with your most luxurious and beautifully-scented shower gel to wash off the grunge and negative energy of your day.
- Dry yourself with a pretty big fluffy towel that you reserve for your special showers before prayer or meditation.
- Massage yourself from head to toe with scented lotion or oil to soften your skin while thinking about how good you feel and wonderful you smell.
- Once done slip into a special outfit that is comfortable enough to sit in for your sacred time.

Now, you are ready to proceed.

Something to Think About:

""Your task is not to seek for love, but merely to find all the barriers within yourself that you have built against it." – Rumi

"I disregard the proportions, the measures, the tempo of the ordinary world. I refuse to live in the ordinary world as an ordinary woman; to enter ordinary relationships. I want ecstasy. I am neurotic... In the sense that I live in my own world, I will not adjust myself to the world. I am adjusted to myself." – Anais Nin

Candles: (Color)	Pink
Incense:	**Suggestions:** **Cafe** – "Perfume of Love" **Essential Essences:** **Summer Solistice –** "Celebration of Life" **Satya Sai Baba:** Nag Champa Agarbatti Your Personal Favorite:
Essential Oil/s	Jasmine, Lavender, Rose, & Vanilla
Moon Cycle:	New moon to the day before full moon
Angel/Spirit Guide:	
Mantras:	
	"I Am grateful. I Am love."
	"I Am the fulfillment of my best dreams & intentions."
	"I Am dedicated to receiving my divine mate."
Notes: (Share your thoughts below)	

"The Sweetest Words"

From my lips flow the most gentle and sweetest words;

They pour out of me intended to bring about maximum healing.

In a way that's gracious and appealing.

Like the nourishing and timeless qualities of honey.

My words are uplifting and can bring unexpected joy; knowing this, I allow myself to relax and be funny.

The positive words I speak build families and create great nations.

Since I understand the power of sacred words and understand that each person I meet is a relation.

If I can say nothing nice,

I will think twice and change my thinking thus, shifting the manner of my speech.

Allowing myself to be true to my goal; **"To be more loving and to truly teach and practice what I preach."**

This is my prayer; so mote it be.

Amen

Cyndi Harris, HP Red Tent Wisdom 2014©

Cyndi's Suggestions:

To really enjoy the full benefits of this beautiful prayer; I recommend you:

- Go into your bedroom and light 2 white candles to start the relaxation process.
- Light some incense or use your diffuser with your favorite essential oil to fragrance your room.
- Turn on your favorite cd or ipod playlist that encourages you to relax and prepare yourself mentally for your upcoming time of communion.
- Also light candles, incense/essential oil diffuser, and music in your bathroom as well.
- Take a shower with your most luxurious and beautifully-scented shower gel to wash off the grunge and negative energy of your day.
- Dry yourself with a pretty big fluffy towel that you reserve for your special showers before prayer or meditation.
- Massage yourself from head to toe with scented lotion or oil to soften your skin while thinking about how good you feel and wonderful you smell.
- Once done slip into a special outfit that is comfortable enough to sit in for your sacred time.

Now, you are ready to proceed.

Something to Think About:

"Your words have the power to heal and uplift a person's life or destroy. Choose your words carefully." – Rev. Cyndi Harris, HP

Candles: (Color)	Pink, Yellow, White
Incense:	**Suggestions:** **Essential Essences: Frankincense and Myrrh** – "Consecration and Healing" **Essential Essences: Love** – "Opening Your Heart" **Satya Sai Baba:** Nag Champa Agarbatti Your Personal Favorite:
Essential Oil/s	Rose, Lavender, Jasmine, and Vanilla
Moon Cycle:	New moon to the day before full moon
Angel/Spirit Guide:	
Mantras:	
	"I Am enjoying the sweetness of love. I graciously receive."
	"I Am enjoying the best in love and romance."
Notes: (Share your thoughts below)	

"Love is…"

Love is light,

Love is right,

When I walk in love, there is no need to fight.

Love is caring,

Love is sharing,

It opens my heart and enables me to be more daring.

Love sustains,

Love eliminates pain,

It brings me joy and once it touches my heart, I will never be the same.

Love is easy,

Love is pleasing,

It is a light within my soul that is never fleeting.

Love is kind,

Love is a sacred gift to exchange between your heart and mine.

Love is the limitless fuel that creates an uplifting and positive place,

A kind and loving space, that negativity and naysayers will never erase.

I am at peace, I am happy, and I AM Love.

This is my prayer. So mote it be. Amen

Cyndi Harris, HP - Red Tent Wisdom 2011©

Cyndi's Suggestions:

To really enjoy the full benefits of this beautiful prayer; I recommend you:

- Go into your bedroom and light 2 white candles to start the relaxation process.
- Light some incense or use your diffuser with your favorite essential oil to fragrance your room.
- Turn on your favorite cd or ipod playlist that encourages you to relax and prepare yourself mentally for your upcoming time of communion.
- Also light candles, incense/essential oil diffuser, and music in your bathroom as well.
- Take a shower with your most luxurious and beautifully-scented shower gel to wash off the grunge and negative energy of your day.
- Dry yourself with a pretty big fluffy towel that you reserve for your special showers before prayer or meditation.
- Massage yourself from head to toe with scented lotion or oil to soften your skin while thinking about how good you feel and wonderful you smell.
- Once done slip into a special outfit that is comfortable enough to sit in for your sacred time.

Now, you are ready to proceed.

Something to Think About:

"Choose peace and watch life's blessings line up to greet you." – Rev. Cyndi Harris, HP

Candles: (Color)	Pink, Red, White
Incense:	**Suggestions:** **Essential Essences: Frankincense and Myrrh** – "Consecration and Healing" **Essential Essences: Love – "Opening Your Heart** **Satya Sai Baba:** Nag Champa Agarbatti Your Personal Favorite:
Essential Oil/s	Jasmine, Lavender
Moon Cycle:	New moon to the day before full moon
Angel/Spirit Guide:	
Mantras:	
	"I Am love."
	"I allow love to be a happy and joy filled experience in my life."
Notes: (Share your thoughts below)	

"2 Hearts – Yours & Mine"

The comfort and warmth of the water flows,

Through its cleansing renewal the fears of our pasts we let go.

A new beginning and loving future we both seek,

Through loving guidance and quiet whispers a cherished and knowledgeable presence speaks.

To walk together with full hearts and open minds,

We thank you for the beauty of discovery and fulfillment we know together we shall find.

This night begins an amazing journey the bringing together of 2 hearts; yours and mine.

Together we move forward without hesitation or worry,

Opening our hearts to contentment, peace, and a precious love,

Which has been blessed with Divine energy and wisdom from above.

This is our prayer, so mote it be.

Cyndi Harris, HP - Red Tent Wisdom 2012© Revised 2014

Cyndi's Suggestions:

To really enjoy the full benefits of this beautiful prayer; I recommend you:

- Go into your bedroom and light 2 white candles to start the relaxation process.
- Light some incense or use your diffuser with your favorite essential oil to fragrance your room.
- Turn on your favorite cd or ipod playlist that encourages you to relax and prepare yourself mentally for your upcoming time of communion.
- Also light candles, incense/essential oil diffuser, and music in your bathroom as well.
- Take a shower with your most luxurious and beautifully-scented shower gel to wash off the grunge and negative energy of your day.
- Dry yourself with a pretty big fluffy towel that you reserve for your special showers before prayer or meditation.
- Massage yourself from head to toe with scented lotion or oil to soften your skin while thinking about how good you feel and wonderful you smell.
- Once done slip into a special outfit that is comfortable enough to sit in for your sacred time.

Now, you are ready to proceed.

Something to Think About:

"Rise above the mundane in order to experience the incredible. 'How do I do this, you ask?' Simply make an active decision to live your best and most positively awesome life." – Rev. Cyndi Harris, HP

Candles: (Color)	Pink, White
Incense:	**Suggestions:** **Egyptian Musk (Whole Foods – Egyptian Goddess)** **Essential Essences: Paris Café** – "Perfume of Love" **Satya Sai Baba:** Nag Champa Agarbatti Your Personal Favorite:
Essential Oil/s	Rose, Lavender, Vanilla, Egyptian Musk
Moon Cycle:	New moon to the day before full moon
Angel/Spirit Guide:	
Mantras:	
	"I Am Love."
	"I Am the loving fulfillment of my best dreams."
Notes: (Share your thoughts below)	

"Divinely Blessed"

My heart and your heart are never far apart.

The love we share, we know is beyond compare,

Life's greatest gift with open hearts we will allow this miraculous shift.

God's perfect plan to unite this loving woman and man,

To be guided by Love Divine,

Everything between us is perfect and absolutely fine.

Each day we move closer to sharing our lives together in complete harmony.

Just as it is meant to be between you and me,

With God's blessing... So mote it be.

Amen

Cyndi Harris, HP - Red Tent Wisdom 2011©

Cyndi's Suggestions:

To really enjoy the full benefits of this beautiful prayer; I recommend you:

- Go into your bedroom and light 2 white candles to start the relaxation process.
- Light some incense or use your diffuser with your favorite essential oil to fragrance your room.
- Turn on your favorite cd or ipod playlist that encourages you to relax and prepare yourself mentally for your upcoming time of communion.
- Also light candles, incense/essential oil diffuser, and music in your bathroom as well.
- Take a shower with your most luxurious and beautifully-scented shower.
- Dry yourself with a pretty big fluffy towel that you reserve for your special showers before prayer or meditation.
- Massage yourself from head to toe with scented lotion or oil to soften your skin while thinking about how good you feel and wonderful you smell.
- Once done slip into a special outfit that is comfortable enough to sit in for your sacred time.

Now, you are ready to proceed.

Something to Think About:

"Life asks, 'Would you like to live an exceptional life; filled with more joy, love, and personal satisfaction?' Your answer, 'Yes, please. I am ready to receive.' Life says, 'Good, I've been waiting for you to come out to play." – Rev. Cyndi Harris, HP

Incense:	**Suggestions:** **Essential Essences:** **Paris Café** - "Perfume of Love" **Balaji Golden Flora** **Satya Sai Baba:** Nag Champa Agarbatti Your Personal Favorite:
Essential Oil/s	Frankincense, Lavender
Moon Cycle:	New moon to the day before full moon
Angel/Spirit Guide:	
Mantras:	
	"I choose to be happily in love each and every day."
	"I give love and allow myself to receive love."
Notes: (Share your thoughts below)	

"Renewed Love"

(name) and (name) will begin once again their loving journey together, As lovers and friends.

This journey will lead them to happy and fulfilling long term marital bliss,

And they seal this desire and longing with a loving and passionate kiss.

Only positive loving actions and thoughts between (name) and (name) will help to create a happy and peaceful relationship that once again feels just right.

This is my humble request tonight.

This is my prayer. So mote it be.

Amen

Cyndi Harris, HP - Red Tent Wisdom 2011©

Cyndi's Suggestions:

To really enjoy the full benefits of this beautiful prayer; I recommend you:

- Go into your bedroom and light 2 white candles to start the relaxation process.
- Light some incense or use your diffuser with your favorite essential oil to fragrance your room.
- Turn on your favorite cd or ipod playlist that encourages you to relax and prepare yourself mentally for your upcoming time of communion.
- Also light candles, incense/essential oil diffuser, and music in your bathroom as well.
- Take a shower with your most luxurious and beautifully-scented shower.
- Dry yourself with a pretty big fluffy towel that you reserve for your special showers before prayer or meditation.
- Massage yourself from head to toe with scented lotion or oil to soften your skin while thinking about how good you feel and wonderful you smell.
- Once done slip into a special outfit that is comfortable enough to sit in for your sacred time.

Now, you are ready to proceed.

Something to Think About:

"Forgiveness truly is a priceless gift you offer yourself. By forgiving others and yourself... You free up blocked energy that can be utilized to live your best life... Right here and right now; do it for yourself and your personal happiness." – Rev. Cyndi Harris, HP

Candles: (Color)	White, Pink
Incense:	**Suggestions:** **Essential Essences: Frankincense and Myrrh** – "Consecration and Healing" **Satya Sai Baba:** Nag Champa Agarbatti Your Personal Favorite:
Essential Oil/s	Frankincense, Myrrh
Moon Cycle:	New moon to the day before full moon
Angel/Spirit Guide:	
Mantras:	
	"I Am forgiveness. I Am forgiven."
	"To be at peace and peaceful is my daily goal."
Notes: (Share your thoughts below)	

"Releasing Old Emotional Bonds"

(Insert Name), this karmic contract between us was created in another time and space.

This contract between us is now void. The time has come to move on to a more positive and rewarding; emotional, mental, and spiritual place.

My karma debt to you is now paid in full; your debt to me is also complete. The etheric chords that bind; are now severed for all times and we are now free. I forgive you and you forgive me.

A happier, more joyful and sweeter life; we each shall live.

This is my prayer, so mote it be.

Amen

Cyndi Harris, HP - Red Tent Wisdom 2012©

Cyndi's Suggestions:

To really enjoy the full benefits of this beautiful prayer; I recommend you:

- Go into your bedroom and light 2 white candles to start the relaxation process.
- Light some incense or use your diffuser with your favorite essential oil to fragrance your room.
- Turn on your favorite cd or ipod playlist that encourages you to relax and prepare yourself mentally for your upcoming time of communion.
- Also light candles, incense/essential oil diffuser, and music in your bathroom as well.
- Take a shower with your most luxurious and beautifully-scented shower.
- Dry yourself with a pretty big fluffy towel that you reserve for your special showers before prayer or meditation.
- Massage yourself from head to toe with scented lotion or oil to soften your skin while thinking about how good you feel and wonderful you smell.
- Once done slip into a special outfit that is comfortable enough to sit in for your sacred time.

Now, you are ready to proceed.

Something to Think About:

"Everything we do is infused with the energy with which we do it. If we are frantic, life will be frantic. If we're peaceful, life will be peaceful. And so our goal in any situation becomes inner peace."
– Marianne Williamson

"Letting go of the past frees you up to live an extraordinary life; filled with happiness, love, and emotional freedom; the type of freedom which allows you to fully and graciously live the life of your best desires and dreams. So, be brave, let go, live without limits." – Rev. Cyndi Harris, HP

Candles: (Color)	Pink, White
Incense:	**Suggestions:** **Essential Essences: Frankincense and Myrrh** – "Consecration and Healing" **Egyptian Musk** **Satya Sai Baba:** Nag Champa Agarbatti Your Personal Favorite:
Essential Oil/s	Frankincense, Myrrh, Lavender
Moon Cycle:	Full moon to the day before new moon
Angel/Spirit Guide:	
Mantras:	
	"I Am forgiveness. I Am emotionally free of everything which no longer best serves me"
	"I release everyone and everything in my life I have emotionally, mentally, physically, and spiritually outgrown."
Notes: (Share your thoughts below)	

"True Love Conquers All"

I pray faithfully and lovingly with confidence that you have brought my Beloved to me.

Disharmony, fear, emotional, mental, and spiritual unrest,

Are now gone forever and we are together.

To each other we only offer our best.

Leaving behind once and for all the energy and any desire for another,

We are deeply in love and truly happy with each other.

Together; safe and protected we have created something special...

A true love; no other will ever disturb.

True peace is ours; we have learned our love truly does conquer all.

This is my prayer. So mote it be.

Amen

Cyndi Harris, HP Red Tent Wisdom 2014©

Cyndi's Suggestions:

To really enjoy the full benefits of this beautiful prayer; I recommend you:

- Go into your bedroom and light 2 white candles to start the relaxation process.
- Light some incense or use your diffuser with your favorite essential oil to fragrance your room.
- Turn on your favorite cd or ipod playlist that encourages you to relax and prepare yourself mentally for your upcoming time of communion.
- Also light candles, incense/essential oil diffuser, and music in your bathroom as well.
- Take a shower with your most luxurious and beautifully-scented shower.
- Dry yourself with a pretty big fluffy towel that you reserve for your special showers before prayer or meditation.
- Massage yourself from head to toe with scented lotion or oil to soften your skin while thinking about how good you feel and wonderful you smell.
- Once done slip into a special outfit that is comfortable enough to sit in for your sacred time.

Now, you are ready to proceed.

Something to Think About:

"Reason is powerless in the expression of love." – Rumi

Candles: (Color)	Pink, White
Incense:	**Suggestions:** **Essential Essences: Love –"Opening Your Heart"** **Satya Sai Baba:** Nag Champa Agarbatti Your Personal Favorite:
Essential Oil/s	Rose, Jasmine, Lavender, Frankincense
Moon Cycle:	New moon to the day before full moon
Angel/Spirit Guide:	
Mantras:	
	"Love is my daily companion and I gratefully receive its' blessings."
	"I trust in the peacefulness and power of true love."
Notes: (Share your thoughts below)	

"The One"

Divine guidance and love which is active in me,

Now manifests my Divinely selected husband/wife for this life.

We enjoy a happy, healthy, loving, and prosperous marriage together,

Here and now!

This is my prayer. So mote it be.

Amen

Cyndi Harris, HP - Red Tent Wisdom 2011©

Candles: (Color)	Pink, Red, White, Purple
Incense:	**Suggestions:** **Essential Essences:** **Love –** "Opening Your Heart" **Essential Essences:** **Prosperity –** Cinnabar & Cinnamon **Satya Sai Baba:** Nag Champa Agarbatti Your Personal Favorite:
Essential Oil/s	Frankincense, Myrrh, Lavender, Rose, Jasmine
Moon Cycle:	New moon to the day before full moon
Angel/Spirit Guide:	
Mantras:	
	"Yes, I say yes to love."
	"I Am receiving the love and joy of my best dreams."
Notes: (Share your thoughts below)	"I Am committed to partnering with my beloved in a long-lasting, loving, passionate, and prosperous romantic relationship."

Chapter 6 - Healing/Health & Well-Being Prayers

The power of prayer has been documented for thousands of years worldwide. The power of positive, purposeful, and uplifting words combined with faith; have the ability to create miracles.

I have seen and personally experienced the healing properties of the right words mixed with belief. Several years ago, I was dealing with the chronic pain of fibromyalgia. Anyone who is currently dealing with this intensely painful condition knows the pain can stop you in your tracks and put your day to day life on hold.

I remember being in so much pain I would cry until my stomach hurt and there where no more tears to shed. The pain was my wake up call to make some life changes since I eventually had to leave my job at a university due to the constant pain and inability to sit or stand for long periods of time.

I knew enough about my body to understand I needed to pay closer attention to my nutrition, rest, and body mechanics. I went to enough specialists to make my head spin and each one was so quick to offer me prescriptions to deal with the symptoms, but there seem to be no real concern to get to the cause of my debilitating pain.

Well, I knew I had no interest in masking the symptoms; my plans where to heal my body in the most complete and natural way.

I did and I am happy to say. I have been totally pain free for about 2 ½ years as of the publication of this book. I went to a few select holistic healers, tracked my nutrition, learned a great deal of information about the nervous system and its care, and stepped deeper into my meditation and prayers.

Meditation and prayers got me through those days the pain made me want to give up, but my faith and understanding that physical issues are usually the manifestation of something deeper and more emotional that a person has been ignoring or neglecting.

I am grateful that I am know walking/talking proof that you can heal yourself when you make a 100% commitment to the journey of wellness.

The following prayers are short and sweet yet highly effective. Use them daily and reclaim your health.

"Restored Physical Health"

My body is a heavenly temple.

Bringing it back into perfect health and Divine balance is simple.

This is my prayer, so mote it be.

Amen

Cyndi Harris, HP - Red Tent Wisdom 2011©

Cyndi's Suggestions:

To really enjoy the full benefits of this beautiful prayer; I recommend you:

- Go into your bedroom and light 2 white candles to start the relaxation process.
- Light some incense or use your diffuser with your favorite essential oil to fragrance your room.
- Turn on your favorite cd or ipod playlist that encourages you to relax and prepare yourself mentally for your upcoming time of communion.
- Also light candles, incense/essential oil diffuser, and music in your bathroom as well.
- Take a shower with your most luxurious and beautifully-scented shower.
- Dry yourself with a pretty big fluffy towel that you reserve for your special showers before prayer or meditation.
- Massage yourself from head to toe with scented lotion or oil to soften your skin while thinking about how good you feel and wonderful you smell.
- Once done slip into a special outfit that is comfortable enough to sit in for your sacred time.

Now, you are ready to proceed.

Something to Think About:

"Love is always the answer to healing of any sort." – Louise Hay

"Personal choice is the "ointment" that heals all things. Why is it so effective? Because, it allows you to confidently retrieve your personal power and make things right in your life." - Rev. Cyndi Harris, HP

Candles: (Color)	Green, Yellow, Blue
Incense:	**Suggestions:** **Essential Essences: Frankincense and Myrrh** – "Consecration and Healing" **Essential Essences: Prosperity** – Cinnabar & Cinnamon **Satya Sai Baba:** Nag Champa Agarbatti Your Personal Favorite:
Essential Oil/s	Frankincense, Myrrh, Lavender
Moon Cycle:	Full moon to the day before new moon
Angel/Spirit Guide:	
Mantras:	
	"I Am healthy. I Am a perfect expression of perfect health."
	"I love being healthy and well; the blessing of perfect health I graciously and gratefully receive."
Notes: (Share your thoughts below)	

"A Healing Blessing"

Instant healing comes easily because in God's Divine Love, I truly believe.

I am gladly open my heart and am willing to receive.

This is my prayer, so mote it be.

Amen

Cyndi Harris, HP - Red Tent Wisdom 2011©

Cyndi's Suggestions:

To really enjoy the full benefits of this beautiful prayer; I recommend you:

- Go into your bedroom and light 2 white candles to start the relaxation process.
- Light some incense or use your diffuser with your favorite essential oil to fragrance your room.
- Turn on your favorite cd or ipod playlist that encourages you to relax and prepare yourself mentally for your upcoming time of communion.
- Also light candles, incense/essential oil diffuser, and music in your bathroom as well.
- Take a shower with your most luxurious and beautifully-scented shower.
- Dry yourself with a pretty big fluffy towel that you reserve for your special showers before prayer or meditation.
- Massage yourself from head to toe with scented lotion or oil to soften your skin while thinking about how good you feel and wonderful you smell.
- Once done slip into a special outfit that is comfortable enough to sit in for your sacred time.

Now, you are ready to proceed.

Something to Think About:

"You are the power in your world! You get to have whatever you choose to think!" – Louise Hay

"Remember to honor yourself in the most peaceful and profound ways possible. You are the keeper of your earthly body temple; its health & well-being are reliant on the choices you make. Choose wisely and with careful consideration of the final outcome of your decisions." Rev. Cyndi Harris, HP

Candles: (Color)	Green
Incense:	**Suggestions:** **Essential Essences:** **Purification** – "Sacred Cedar and Lavender" **Satya Sai Baba:** Nag Champa Agarbatti Your Personal Favorite:
Essential Oil/s	Frankincense, Myrrh
Moon Cycle:	New moon to the day before full moon
Angel/Spirit Guide:	
Mantras:	
	"Perfect health and well-being I graciously receive. Peace of mind is part of my wellness destiny."
Notes: (Share your thoughts below)	

"A Prayer of Release - Choose Love"

Allow the negativity to come to light,

This will allow us to correct this situation and make things right.

Any ill wishes must now be gone,

For they can no longer do any harm.

And the one who is creating any ill wishes must now move on.

Only actions and words that encourage everyone's best and highest good,

Helps to return the harmony and love for everyone as it should.

This is my prayer. So mote it be.

Cyndi Harris, HP - Red Tent Wisdom 2011©

Cyndi's Suggestions:

To really enjoy the full benefits of this beautiful prayer; I recommend you:

- Go into your bedroom and light 2 white candles to start the relaxation process.
- Light some incense or use your diffuser with your favorite essential oil to fragrance your room.
- Turn on your favorite cd or ipod playlist that encourages you to relax and prepare yourself mentally for your upcoming time of communion.
- Also light candles, incense/essential oil diffuser, and music in your bathroom as well.
- Take a shower with your most luxurious and beautifully-scented shower.
- Dry yourself with a pretty big fluffy towel that you reserve for your special showers before prayer or meditation.
- Massage yourself from head to toe with scented lotion or oil to soften your skin while thinking about how good you feel and wonderful you smell.
- Once done slip into a special outfit that is comfortable enough to sit in for your sacred time.

Now, you are ready to proceed.

Something to Think About:

"When faced with a difficult person or situation choice love; even if they continue to act out on a soulful level your loving wisdom has been received." - Rev. Cyndi Harris, HP

"Holding on to anger is a dangerous waste of time and precious life energy that you could be using to enjoy yourself and helping others. Allow anger to have its moment, but choose your words carefully since your goal is to move on without any clinging energetic residue." Rev. Cyndi Harris, HP

Candles: (Color)	Green, Black, White
Incense:	**Suggestions:** **Essential Essences: Frankincense and Myrrh** – "Consecration and Healing" **Satya Sai Baba:** Nag Champa Agarbatti Your Personal Favorite:
Essential Oil/s	Frankincense, Myrrh
Moon Cycle:	Full moon to the day before new moon
Angel/Spirit Guide:	
Mantras:	
	"I forgive and I Am forgiven."
	"I live my life in the most loving way."
Notes: (Share your thoughts below)	

"Zero Effects – I AM Free."

I am protected from other people's drama.

Its draining and negative energy have ZERO effect on me.

I am totally loved and my day is filled with peace.

My day progresses with the greatest of ease.

This is my prayer, so mote it be.

Amen

Cyndi Harris, HP - Red Tent Wisdom 2011©

Cyndi's Suggestions:

To really enjoy the full benefits of this beautiful prayer; I recommend you:

- Go into your bedroom and light 2 white candles to start the relaxation process.
- Light some incense or use your diffuser with your favorite essential oil to fragrance your room.
- Turn on your favorite cd or ipod playlist that encourages you to relax and prepare yourself mentally for your upcoming time of communion.
- Also light candles, incense/essential oil diffuser, and music in your bathroom as well.
- Take a shower with your most luxurious and beautifully-scented shower.
- Dry yourself with a pretty big fluffy towel that you reserve for your special showers before prayer or meditation.
- Massage yourself from head to toe with scented lotion or oil to soften your skin while thinking about how good you feel and wonderful you smell.
- Once done slip into a special outfit that is comfortable enough to sit in for your sacred time.

Now, you are ready to proceed.

Something to Think About:

"Your opinion of yourself is the only one that matters. Stop allowing others to decide how much or little you will receive from living your life. It has been and always will be your choice to be, do, and receive more from life. Be fearless and go for more." - Rev. Cyndi Harris, HP

Candles: (Color)	White, Black
Incense:	**Suggestions:** **Essential Essences:** **Purification –** "Sacred Cedar & Lavender" **Satya Sai Baba:** Nag Champa Agarbatti Your Personal Favorite:
Essential Oil/s	Frankincense, Myrrh
Moon Cycle:	Full moon to the day before new moon
Angel/Spirit Guide:	
Mantras:	
	"I Am relaxed."
	"Life only brings the best people and situations to me. I joyfully receive."
Notes: (Share your thoughts below)	

Chapter 7 - Improved Communication Prayer

Open, honest, and productive conversation is important in all of our relationships. Whether we are talking to our lover, husband, children, parents, siblings, co-workers, etc; understanding how to effectively and eloquently express yourself is vital to the health and well-being of these relationships.

Unfortunately, effective communication is something very few people ever see modeled from their childhood into adulthood. And as adults if we never truly learned how to speak up and be clear about our desires and needs. We will wind up in situation after situation that is challenging and unfulfilling.

Passive/Aggressive behavior is a perfect example of an inability to communicate confidently. Instead of speaking up and saying what needs to be said; a passive/aggressive person will say nothing and over time begin to resent the people or situations in their lives.

And the people around them will have no idea why this person is so unhappy. It is an unproductive and hurtful cycle that can negatively affect many people.

Fear is another block to great communication. If a person is afraid of ridicule, unpleasant verbal confrontations, or receiving the silent treatment for speaking up; fear sets in and peace of mind is compromised.

The prayer in this section was created to offer you encouraging words to speak and remind you that you can release anyone who you feel is blocking your ability to live at your full potential.

"Speaking Your Truth"

I have found my voice…

And in all things affecting me, I have a choice.

I fully embrace my personal power.

Negativity and other people's drama no longer cause me to sit back and cower.

I AM strong…

And I allow no one in my personal space that no longer belongs.

This is my prayer, so mote it be.

Amen

Cyndi Harris, HP - Red Tent Wisdom 2011©

Cyndi's Suggestions:

To really enjoy the full benefits of this beautiful prayer; I recommend you:

- Go into your bedroom and light 2 white candles to start the relaxation process.
- Light some incense or use your diffuser with your favorite essential oil to fragrance your room.
- Turn on your favorite cd or ipod playlist that encourages you to relax and prepare yourself mentally for your upcoming time of communion.
- Also light candles, incense/essential oil diffuser, and music in your bathroom as well.
- Take a shower with your most luxurious and beautifully-scented shower.
- Dry yourself with a pretty big fluffy towel that you reserve for your special showers before prayer or meditation.
- Massage yourself from head to toe with scented lotion or oil to soften your skin while thinking about how good you feel and wonderful you smell.
- Once done slip into a special outfit that is comfortable enough to sit in for your sacred time.

Now, you are ready to proceed.

Something to Think About:

"You are more powerful than you know. Life is only filled with obstacles if you choose to be defeated. Instead of expecting to be disappointed; choose to experience each moment as a stepping stone to greater and more fulfilling life success then, watch how quickly your blessings unfold before you." Rev. Cyndi Harris, HP

Candles: (Color)	Yellow
Incense:	**Suggestions:** **Satya Sai Baba:** Nag Champa Agarbatti Your Personal Favorite:
Essential Oil/s	Tea Tree Oil
Moon Cycle:	Full moon to the day before new moon
Angel/Spirit Guide:	
Mantras:	
	"I Am awesome."
	"People treat me with the upmost respect."
Notes: (Share your thoughts below)	

Chapter 8 - Peaceful Living Prayers

Living a peaceful soul-satisfying life that increases the joy and prosperity in our life is possible. To do so requires a commitment to making positive choices, forgiving the past, and deciding to receive the blessings you continuously ask for.

Yes, learning to allow and receive is a huge part of living a peaceful and joyous life. Our irrational habit of hitting the proverbial "brakes" causes more stress and strife than we want to admit.

The cycle starts; I'll use dating as an example.

You decide you are ready to meet a great guy after being single for a several months.

First the questions:

Should I put a profile online? One of the girls at work met a great guy and now she is planning her wedding.

But, one of my friends did online dating and she had an awful experience and hasn't dated anyone new in over a year. She says most guys online are predators looking for someone to take care of them. Her date didn't bring his wallet and she had to pay for their drinks and meals. She thinks I should just stay single.

This debate can go on for months and you never really get around to dating even though you are tired of being alone, but you are worried that you would upset your friend if you didn't take her online dating advise seriously.

And, it goes on and on. You are stressed out for no real reason and your life remains uneventful and mundane. You have no peace because, you are living in fear;

refusing to make any committed decisions which could lead you to the very love and happiness you are seeking.

The above scenario is only a sample of the various ways people sabotage their lives and peace of mind. Being clear about your desires and dreams is the first step to real happiness.

The following prayer is a personal freedom anthem. Use it daily before you leave the house to empower your day.

"Peace of Mind"

I allow myself the freedom to be me.

I now release those who choose to criticize me; I am comfortable just letting them be.

I gladly relinquish the need to always be right.

I give up the need to become defensive and ready to fight; feelings that cause me to feel unsettled and undo fright.

I open up my heart this night to receive the blessing of peace of mind.

My spirit feels free, happy, and is filled with absolute delight.

This is my prayer, so mote it be.

Amen

Cyndi Harris, HP - Red Tent Wisdom 2012© Revised 2014

Cyndi's Suggestions:

To really enjoy the full benefits of this beautiful prayer; I recommend you:

- Go into your bedroom and light 2 white candles to start the relaxation process.
- Light some incense or use your diffuser with your favorite essential oil to fragrance your room.
- Turn on your favorite cd or ipod playlist that encourages you to relax and prepare yourself mentally for your upcoming time of communion.
- Also light candles, incense/essential oil diffuser, and music in your bathroom as well.
- Take a shower with your most luxurious and beautifully-scented shower.
- Dry yourself with a pretty big fluffy towel that you reserve for your special showers before prayer or meditation.
- Massage yourself from head to toe with scented lotion or oil to soften your skin while thinking about how good you feel and wonderful you smell.
- Once done slip into a special outfit that is comfortable enough to sit in for your sacred time.

Now, you are ready to proceed.

Something to Think About:

"There is nothing enlightened about shrinking so that other people wouldn't feel insecure around you. We are all meant to shine, as children do." – Marianne Williamson

"Only you can give yourself permission to be your personal best. Everyone who believes in you is simply a cheerleader whose encouragement and support helps to light your way. You and you alone must do the work." - Rev. Cyndi Harris, HP

Candles: (Color)	Green Yellow, White
Incense:	
Essential Oil/s	Lavender
Moon Cycle:	Full moon to the day before new moon
Angel/Spirit Guide:	
Mantras:	
	"I Am living my best life ever because, I appreciate who I Am."
Notes: (Share your thoughts below)	

I suffer no more... I AM Free

I AM free and I rejoice in being me.

I AM free and I AM at peace with being me.

I AM free and I love being me.

As I live my life each day; I understand my past is not my complete story.

I use it as a stepping stone to successfully live my life and flourish in the value of each day's glory.

I no longer feel, alone, and out of place.

I step fully into my life; receiving more love and joy while living in Divine Grace.

I AM at peace because, I AM free and I Love being me.

This is my prayer. So mote it be.

Amen

Cyndi Harris, HP – Red Tent Wisdom 2014©

Cyndi's Suggestions:

To really enjoy the full benefits of this beautiful prayer; I recommend you:

- Go into your bedroom and light 2 white candles to start the relaxation process.
- Light some incense or use your diffuser with your favorite essential oil to fragrance your room.
- Turn on your favorite cd or ipod playlist that encourages you to relax and prepare yourself mentally for your upcoming time of communion.
- Also light candles, incense/essential oil diffuser, and music in your bathroom as well.
- Take a shower with your most luxurious and beautifully-scented shower.
- Dry yourself with a pretty big fluffy towel that you reserve for your special showers before prayer or meditation.
- Massage yourself from head to toe with scented lotion or oil to soften your skin while thinking about how good you feel and wonderful you smell.
- Once done slip into a special outfit that is comfortable enough to sit in for your sacred time.

Now, you are ready to proceed.

Something to Think About:

"Choose peace and watch life's blessings line up to greet you."
Rev. Cyndi Harris, HP

Candles: (Color)	White
Incense:	**Suggestions:** **Essential Essences: Frankincense and Myrrh** – "Consecration and Healing" **Satya Sai Baba:** Nag Champa Agarbatti Your Personal Favorite:
Essential Oil/s	Frankincense
Moon Cycle:	New moon to the day before full moon
Angel/Spirit Guide:	
Mantras:	
	"I Am Peaceful. I Am at peace with my life."
Notes: (Share your thoughts below)	

Chapter 9 - Sacred Femininity Prayers

This chapter is my favorite part of this book. It focuses on the beauty and sacred wisdom of being a woman.

In a world that continues to diminish a woman's worth in society. I wrote these poems/prayers as a reminder that each of us is a vital part of the circle of life. Whether you had a child/children or not; every human life must come through a woman; every one of us was nurtured, cuddled, and protected by a woman.

Whether your mom was wonderful or a disaster; you must admit without her you would not be here. So, as we take a few moments in this chapter to reflect on the sacredness of women. I hope you will use these prayers to add more confidence and purpose to what you do and how you live your life.

The very nature of womanhood is about creation and bringing life, possibilities, and visions into reality. There can be no guilt or shame around the blessings and privilege of womanhood. We must remember who we are and pass this information on to the men, children, and other women in our lives; encouraging each other as we continue to rid ourselves of the emotional and mental "trash" that has been weighing us down.

We are the seat of creation; hold your head up, walk with confidence, and reclaim your wisdom.

"I AM the Seat of Creation"

I Am the seat of creation, I Am the mother of every nation.

I Am sacred, I Am sure.

My thoughts, intentions, and Love are pure.

I Am humble, I Am Great.

The wisdom that I carry, I have grown to appreciate.

I Am Wombman, I Am strong.

Leading others to abundance, health, and well-being is where I belong.

I Am eternal wisdom, I Am wise.

I graciously embrace and love myself and refuse to live any more lies.

I Am heavenly-made; graciously & humbly blessed... I remember who I Am. The illusion that I am unworthy has begun to fade.

I choose to live my life to the fullest. Thus, allowing me to offer others and my heavenly parents... My very best.

This is my prayer; so mote it be.

Amen

Cyndi Harris – Red Tent Wisdom 2014©

Cyndi's Suggestions:

To really enjoy the full benefits of this beautiful prayer; I recommend you:

- Go into your bedroom and light 2 white candles to start the relaxation process.
- Light some incense or use your diffuser with your favorite essential oil to fragrance your room.
- Turn on your favorite cd or ipod playlist that encourages you to relax and prepare yourself mentally for your upcoming time of communion.
- Also light candles, incense/essential oil diffuser, and music in your bathroom as well.
- Take a shower with your most luxurious and beautifully-scented shower.
- Dry yourself with a pretty big fluffy towel that you reserve for your special showers before prayer or meditation.
- Massage yourself from head to toe with scented lotion or oil to soften your skin while thinking about how good you feel and wonderful you smell.
- Once done slip into a special outfit that is comfortable enough to sit in for your sacred time.

Now, you are ready to proceed.

Something to Think About:

"Unlock your personal wisdom. You are Divinely created to be a blessing to yourself and others who have the pleasure of meeting you." - Rev. Cyndi Harris, HP

"Love is what we are born with. Fear is what we learn. The spiritual journey is the unlearning of fear and prejudices and the acceptance of love back into our hearts. Love is the essential reality and our purpose on earth... to experience love in ourselves and others, is the meaning of life. Meaning does not lie in things. Meaning lies in us." – Marianne Williamson

Candles: (Color)	Green, Pink
Incense:	**Suggestions:** **Essential Essences: Frankincense and Myrrh** – "Consecration and Healing" **Essential Essences: Prosperity** – Cinnabar & Cinnamon **Satya Sai Baba:** Nag Champa Agarbatti Your Personal Favorite:
Essential Oil/s	Rose, Lavender
Moon Cycle:	New moon to the day before full moon
Angel/Spirit Guide:	
Mantras:	
	"I happily honor my inner wisdom."
	"I Am full of charm and grace; miracles happen here."
Notes: (Share your thoughts below)	

And finally, here's a special treat to bring us to the conclusion of our series of poems and prayers I have included a simple yet effective ritual for you to enjoy.

"Sweet Results"

Today (Insert Name) is being generous, kind, thoughtful, and sweet.

I am grateful for this show of generosity; the good feelings and shared joy are pleasant and upbeat.

Thank you (Insert Name), I appreciate you and all you do for me.

This is my prayer; so mote it be... Amen

Cyndi Harris, Red Tent Wisdom 2014©

Instructions:

Prepare a cup of herbal tea (Ideally chamomile) and add 1Tbs. (1 teaspoon if you are diabetic... **nothing artificial**... the sweetness must be real) of honey. Real maple syrup works too.

As you are stirring in the honey/maple syrup say this prayer.

Then, relax and enjoy your cup of tea thinking about the happy outcome of your request.

Once done... Proceed with the rest of your day.

Well, this is the end of our special guide to successfully starting a basic, but effective sacred wisdom and gratitude practice. I hope you will enjoy this information as much as I enjoyed creating it for you.

Sacred ceremonies are blessings in disguise and creating then, enjoying sacred space within your home will gradually change the dynamics of your life and the lives of those closest to you. Share the joy.

The path to a peaceful mind and total well-being begins with a commitment to your wellness and setting aside time each day to do things that enrich your body, mind, and spirit. Be consistent and reap the benefits you deserve.

As you move along this magical path I am wishing you much love and unlimited joy.

Have an incredible day,

Cyndi Harris, HP

Irresistible Living Coach at Cyndi's Red Tent Wisdom

www.redtentwisdom.com

Appendix 1

Candle Color Definitions

Here is a brief description of candles and the most popular colors used for sacred ceremonies.

Candle Definitions:

Green:

Abundance, growth, money, success, wealth, physical healing, health, marriage, fertility, employment, balance, stimulates growth, healing, financial success, good luck, new job.

Gold:

Enlightenment, protection, success, wealth, money, masculinity, playfulness, divination, victory, enhances communication; Useful in ceremonies to attract good fortune and/or money.

Yellow:

Communication, wisdom, action, inspiration, creativity, memory enhancer, attraction, confidence, energy, cheerfulness, endurance, stability and security.

Red:

Energy, vitality, and strength, health, passion, sex, love, protection, fertility, fast action, strength, potency, lust, blood, courage, energy, attraction, magnetism, desire, physical strength, power.

Pink:

Devotion, love, friendship, romance, honor, spiritual healing, caring, affection, forming partnerships, peace, emotional healing, Universal love, purest form of love, love that is unconditional, spiritual love without sexual overtures, raises vibrations (your own and others), sensitivity, healing.

Blue:

Communication, truth, peace, wisdom, protection, harmony,

inspiration, patience, health, happiness, luck, communication, loyalty, peaceful, cooling, contentment, healing, devotion, meditation.

Purple:

Use with white candle to neutralize effects of karma. Ancient wisdom, the third eye, meditation, spirituality, success, confidence, hidden knowledge, protection, divination, all forms of expansion, use to manifest what you want, spiritual protection, power, wisdom, healing.

Violet:

Encourages strength, success, ideal for rituals designed to secure ambition, independence, prosperity, to establish a deeper connection with the spiritual world.

Lavender/Lilac:

Manifestation, spirituality, compassion, enhances understanding, make contact with Higher-Self, to attract spiritual assistance, encourages relaxation.

Orange:

Cleanses negative attitudes, situations and places, brings happiness, attracts good things into your life, power, luck, warmth, energy building, enthusiasm, attracts success and prosperity, emotional healing, attracts friends, courage and ambition.

Brown:

Use in ceremonies for material gain, eliminates indecisiveness, enhances concentration. Expands financial success, material prosperity, home, friendships, balance, earth magic, improves concentration, wealth, success, stability.

Black:

Burning black with any other color dissolves negative energies, used for protection, banishing. Also used to enhance the healing of powerful illnesses.

White:

The balance of all colors; spiritual enlightenment, clairvoyance, healing, innocence, clarity and unity, purification, peace, truth, protection, cleansing, repels negativity; use to bring peace; heals emotions, and provides protection.

Note: White can be used in place of any other candle color and is suitable for any ritual.

Appendix 2

Supply Websites and Links

Incenses can be used during ceremonies for love, forgiveness, abundance, courage, healing, and so much more. You can use certain scents for specific ceremonies or private meditations. The suggestions offered in this book are recommendations and ones I personally use.

To stay in the spirit of creating sacred space and ceremonies; buy a decorative box to keep them in and keep a journal on which incense you used to enhance your ceremonies or add fragrance to your home.

This is your journey so make it special.

To get you started, in this section I have included some of my favorite scents and brands. I know some people may be sensitive to certain types of incenses. There are certain types that give me a headache. So, I am sure it happens to others as well.

Personally, generally, I am unable to use any type of black colored incense; something about the charcoal base gives me a headache.

But, you may be different so, use this list as a starter and be bold and try different types. There are:

- Japanese
- Tibetan
- Eastern Indian
- African
- And so many other types of incenses to choose from.

You can purchase them in many different forms:

- Cones
- Resins
- Powders
- And sticks.

I personally use sticks and resins (in large rooms or outside)

Experiment and see which ones work best for you.

Irresistible and Intoxicating Incenses - The List:

1. **Balaji Golden Flora** – Smells delightful. It has a rich and sensual floral/spicy scent.
2. **Satya Sai Baba – Nag Champa Agarbatti**
3. **Om Nag Champa**
4. **Escential Essences:**
   a. **Frankincense and Myrrh** – "Consecration and Healing"
   b. **Love** – "Opening Your Heart"
   c. **Paris Café** – "Perfume of Love"
   d. **Prosperity** – "Cinnabar and Cinnamon"
   e. **Purification** – "Sacred Cedar and Lavender"
   f. **Summer Solistice** – "Celebration of Life"
5. **Song of India** – India Temple Incenses (I prefer the cones, the sticks give me a migraine, but the sticks may work for you.)
   a. And many more… check out this website for these and more fragrances: http://www.mysticunicorn.com/escentialsticks.html
6. **Egyptian Musk** (Also sold at Whole Foods as "Egyptian Goddess)
7. **Another great website:** http://incenseontheway.com They have a wide variety of options from incenses from sticks (regular and large garden size) to powders/resins, burners, and more)

Hopefully, the list and websites are enough to peak your curiosity.

ABOUT THE AUTHOR

Rev. Cyndi Harris is a woman who believes in living life fully; embracing and recognizing the beauty, joy, and wisdom that is the birthright of every woman.

For far too long women have been trying to find their rightful, most dynamic, and powerful place in life. Cyndi is:

• An advocate
• Advisor/Coach
• Author
• Facilitator
• Shoulder to cry on
• And your biggest cheerleader when it is time to celebrate your success.

She is the one who will help you reawaken your intuition/inner wise woman insights and rediscover how to reclaim your best and most satisfying desires and dreams. She will help you move from stagnation to creation then intention which will finally lead you to completion.

And in the process you will learn to how to graciously surrender to the life blessings and miracles that have been waiting for you.

For more information about: Rev. Cyndi or to learn about additional services and products.

Go to: **www.redtentwisdom.com**

Made in the USA
San Bernardino,
CA